- For Tim and Paul
  with my love

contents

birdbath   1
the storm   2
autumn walk   3
ending   4
the gulf war show   5
peace   6
living up to a label   7
words; hope   8
dying mother   9
happiness I   10
after the divorce   11
night thoughts   12
the necklace   14

birds   16
nightmare christmas   17
solitude   18
marriage   19
aids victim   20
unloving; infatuation   21
happiness II   22
a new puppy   23
richmond park   24
life force   26
the house   27
famine in africa   28
bangladesh cyclone   29
in memory of an old dog   30
the scream   32
my young self   33
the garden   34
understanding   36
love   37
the day you leave hospital   38
depression   39
cards in the afternoon   40
thoughts about death   42
breakdown   44
swan in winter   45
my father   46
mourning the loss of christian faith   47
the fool's hour   48

birdbath

Catch it on the moment
Fleeting whirl of feathers
Dipping, cautious, delicate
Beak into the waters,
Cascading flutter of drops
Small body gyrating as a dancer
Then upwards over
The trees cover
Sunlight on the wings,
Away from the autumn garden.
Enough, he is gone
Into someone else's future;
And we who have known
The blackness of the cold
Night's edge smile.....
Knowing that nothing is
Quite as beautiful
Or as desperate
As it would seem.

the storm

Like bodies after battle they lie
The fallen trees.
Strewn across the dying wood lifeless
Leaves caught in the wreckage of the place,
New vistas spawned by the ravaging storm.
Huge shallow roots gawp at the sky
Desolate, abandoned by the earth itself.
Their lives cut short, a massive coronary
Cracking, groaning, piling one upon the other
Seized by the dervish wind
All that was not strong enough
Falling to it's turbulent whiplash.
Broken, brought to the ground
Snapped like a pencil.
Your solid trunk in a shifting world
Epitomises all that is stable,
Your green and tender buds in spring
Our own hope of renewal.
No wonder we feel, standing in the broken wood
A hideous sense of loss.

autumn walk

Wild stags bellow their needs
Across the empty hillside,
In frenzied activity
Jostling for power
Among their gentle harem.

I walk along the hill path
Through open woods
As autumn falls
Turning the summer place
Into a tangle of branches,

Slashed with golden lights.
Squirrels taunt my terrier
To ever closer chase, sensing
They will always get away.
Eyes shining, ears alert,

She still pursues, undaunted.
The hunter's high is strong
In the dying year.
Birds, large as dreams
Flush out of the bushes

Lifting my heart away, high
On the fickle wind.
Sensitive wide eyed as
A virgin bride, the doe steps
Delicately across my path,

Then comes another gently
Graceful, speeding away
Triumphant stag in all his glory
Following in keen pursuit.
Flushed, muddy, full of mindless hope

For what I do not know or
Why it should be, that
Days to come seem less
Perilously grave, for having had
Those moments on an autumn walk.

ending

It cannot last; it has been said,
The moment frozen on air.
Clods in the mind whisper,

The old tinker's on the road again
Jangling with the weight of it.
Like a bough in frosting gale

My heart dips and sways
Drawn always to your presence.
While on the door of our impassioned

Time, hope beats like a wild
Bird, our silences filled
With echoes of parting.

the gulf war show

If only they were less splendid
Those killing machines....

Huge metal sculptures
Riding magnificently
Across the waters to war.
Phallic guns at the ready,

Symmetry of decks purposeful, satisfying,
High technology compacted
Into elegant grey steel.
Screaming engines taking off

Into shimmering desert sky,
Arrogant Gods of power
Thrilling in their domination of space.
Massive caterpillars sliding with

Monstrous certainty over
Cruel desert terrain.
If only they had no beauty at all
Those killing machines,

We might not be seduced
By their masculine appeal
As each goes to its task
In disciplined orderly fashion.

We still feel a thrill despite ourselves,
Momentarily forgetting our sons and lovers
Impotently caught up in the coil
Of their nightmarish purposes.

peace

Birds call faintly singing
On the smothered day
Soft as rain, summer dusting leaves,

Shadows pitch onto meadows.
Dales, confusing greenery
Into a welter of shades.

Skies open wide promising
Much in their translucent void.
So must we grow in time.

Sitting near the edge;
waiting on a hill
Drowning in the day's long sleep.

living up
to a label

My son of five said
"What are you writing?"
"A poem" I said, for want of a word.
"What's it about your poem?" he asked me.
"You" I said, to make it quite clear.
He nodded then, all wise understanding,
That was quite right and just as it should be,
So he settled down then to watch television
With a look that implied,
What a nice old world

Next day his teacher said
"I hear you're a poet."
What had I done to be labelled that way?
A few scribbled lines on odd scraps of paper
Thoughts that built up and had to be free,
Impressions, feelings too hard to handle,
Guilty escapes from domesticity.

How could I hope to live up to that image?
To be a real poet is no easy task,
Yet how could I let this small boy down
When he told his teacher with such loving pride.
The only hope was to make the thing valid
At least he'd feel I'd not lied.
So "yes" I said, out straight to his teacher.
But on the way home how I sighed.

words

There is a gentle harmony in words
as they gather and flow, dancing to
their own rhythm shaping a thousand
life impressions into a neat package
on the page. As carefully wrapped as
a birthday parcel they are things to
work on when the world's askew,
scalpel sharp, they wound and heal,
    weaving muddled emotions into
    plaits of reasonable harmony.

hope

Wait in the still moment for a sign
That in the hopeless night's core
A voice may finally be heard.
Not necessarily intellectual,
Nor deep with paradox or emotion
Or cool with the precision
Of scientific truth.
Yet one in which they might have echoes
Ringing from each other
In a short clear note.

dying mother

In lines they lie, bodies without grace
Uttering grunts and cries, incontinent crevices
Looked after with all clinical care.

She lies - my mother - fourth on the right
Clear soft skin, cheekbones high,
Hair pulled back from her proud old face.

Eyesight nearly gone she does not see
The kind black nurse who treats her like a child,
The lino, the other beds, or smells the disinfectant,

or lavender cologne with which I wipe her head.
The sudden call or helpless groan
Mercifully she cannot hear

Until her hearing aid is on
And I then shout into her ear,
Her world a silent place.

How to offer balm to this old soul
Who lived with courage for so long.
Ninety years is no divide and all

The modern ways she takes
Broad-minded in her stride.
She taught me nothing practical,

Because she is not so,
But searching and philosophy
And how to just keep on.

happiness

Butterflies in the hedgerows dance
And all is rounded with the summertime.
From the downs the air sea drenched
Brings hope that such completion will endure,
Winter not encroach upon the lane.
For in the lane time is still, the moment
Quite unspoiled by fearful probabilities.

He walks towards me where I stand
My love, wrapped in the pulsing day,
Simple as a singing bird.
So joyful then, so full of hope am I,
Knowing that against such things
Tomorrows tears cannot intrude.

after
the divorce

We walked, my son and I
Stripling crackle of leaves under foot
The sky a deep wild gold,
Autumn at her most majestic turn

High up a hill.
"Is there really any point to life?"
He said.
Already having seen the harsh and ugly

Override the good.
I could only manage
"Look...look at all the beauty."
Perhaps he understood.

When he returned to boarding school that night
I sat in the car and cried,
The windows of the houses seemed to stare
With glittering empty eyes as I passed.

night thoughts

Before the dawn,
When darkness
Is in sole command

And sleeping minds
Empty the day's refuse
Into the bin of night,

Before the first feathered call
That light will come again
Fear hovers for the wide awake.

On to the mind's landscape
The sick and suffering crowd,
Their panic and their pain are yours

Wrapped in their inescapable fate
Lonely as a moon.
Withered babies

Starving wide eyed
Under the scorching sun.
Scrawny parents helpless

Part of the barren waste.
If only something
Inevitable as death

Could be eschewed with grace,
Dropping the leaves of our transient lives
In a golden glory, without agony.

Imagination has it's chains
Though it bid us fly,
So in the blackest hour

We collapse at the grave
Of all our hopes.
Yet as a dancer when the music fades

Still pirouettes until the dance is done
We tense and twirl, though the song is gone.
Candles in an empty church burn out

Prayer lingers on...

the necklace

Sometimes I take great gulps of beauty,
Storing it to act as blubber
Against harsh cold of ugliness,
And like a squirrel hoard it
In some secret place,
Those nuggets of light
Against the dark.
Forest walks filled with scent of pine,
Small sun filled glades in which to lie and talk.
Or wrapped up warm along the old sea wall
Miles of marshes where sea birds play.

And small boats battle with wind and rain,
The sun a crimson ball behind the reeds.
An empty stage, the audience gone
Music echoing on the air.
I've done it and I'm seventeen.
Those long hard years and bloody toes
A ballet dancer now... a pro.
Swoonings and fallings into love
Delirious moments, heady stuff,
While secret looks from wings reveal
A conspiracy of lust.

Alive as never quite before,
You drown in the emotion.
Diminutive fingers and toes,
Warm smelling bundle of baby
Sleeping happy in your arms,
The answer you've been waiting for,
Missing piece of the puzzle.
A garden caught between sea and sky
Lost in the pulsing heat.
Swimming gently in the ice clear water
Bougainvillia and hibiscus

Bedazzling the eyes.
Or eating in the cool of evening
In some exotic little port,
With the one you love,
Tipsy with the sun and air.
Each has their own jewels
To cherish and maintain
Special to themselves alone.
A necklace to wear in those dark times,
When all else seems gone
Your life quite bare.

birds

Shadowy lawn alive with feathered life hopping,
Flicking, picking at grasses, searching for grubs.
Starlings, sparrows, woodpigeon, magpies, drop
Through trees urgently squabbling
For their turn at the water bowl,
Enveloping the garden space.

Entering their world, I feel released
imagining their kind, air locked in dreams,
Scoffing at the earth bound across oceans' fall.
Over tangled wilderness they come again
Small pulsing breast beneath a silken canopy
Feathered strands batting the airways.

Eagles, in those high and lonely places
Lost in mountain mist, swoop to their prey.
White sea birds skim above land's edge,
Among battered cliffs they loom in calling,
Linking us to our secret selves
Following magic courses, deep compelling,

We almost sense them wakening from our dreams.
Small bird, carry my hopes high; shimmer
With the wind across your airborne life.
Dancing with the day's delight, singing
Your song at dawn as I meditate.

nightmare
christmas

You drink alone in the light
Of the last candle flame.
Drowning the pain, as your hope

Seeps away. Love, it would seem,
All crushed in the space of a tantrum.
Part of life irrevocably spoiled.

Tree, fairy lights, baubles twinkling,
Holly, cards, shining silver.
Food, wine, to feast and cheer with.

So much time and love went to it.
What blind cause breaks families apart,
UnChristlike Christmas day.

Sudden irritation in the heat of the moment,
Words spoken too soon, not vetted enough,
Driving into caverns of fear, resentment,

Cruel disharmonies, ugly vibrations.
Alone in your desert
The feast of hope gone.

The baby lies withered
Under bright star
Stillborn in the manger.

solitude

Rare moments, valuable and sustaining
In which to illuminate shadows of
Pent up despair, unravel the
Unsung story of your days and
Penetrate the fortress of your fears.
Awash in silence, mending the hurts, the
Humiliations that silly people can bestow
In jealous self centred greed
Upon each others psyche.
Recharge those power houses that lie within,
Although at times so very dimly,
Of courage, creativity, awareness.
Why then do we fear your mantle
Flicking wavelengths, pushing knobs
Joining in the screech of voices
With such frenetic zeal.

marriage

Does unhappiness outweigh the joy
Bickering, the calm,
Worry, the harmony,
Frustration, the satisfaction,
Compromise, the settlement?

Perhaps not, for we are
Together in the early hours,
The solid comfort of your
Presence is good.

Expecting little,
Illusions gone.
Accepting frailty,
Peace is possible.
Old age of emotion in
Middle aged bodies.

So now, at the thought of your absence
I know I would miss you,
A great emptiness would there be there,
An ugly deprivation.

aids victim

Some see you as a leper,
Those righteous, rigid.
Looking haunted, starved,
Eyes luminous with pain.
You know you are not
Lovely any more. An aura
Of horror surrounds your
Broken frame; fear is on
The air that you expel.
Illness's evil magnified,
By eyes filled with pitying
Reproach. You were, not so
Long ago, wrapped warm
In shawls and Mother's arms.
Fingers and toes all plumped.
Your infant heart beat
Fast in love. You lived
As your nature called.
Now as you wait to die,
God in you sing, so that
Falling through eternity,
Reaching stars, touching
The sun's edge, you laugh
At the bad joke.

unloving

What angry desolation when the
Ability to love is drained from within.
Seeping like a wound, dredging the heart,
Until bloodless, guts drawn out,
Parched as a crisp, scarred by indifference,
Meaningless activity takes over.
Seditious thoughts permeate
Landscape that is without core
Or signpost, barren ground of your being
Laid bare to wearisome coldness,
A traveller far from home.

infatuation

Go summer love, I must not keep you any more,
Fantasy will not fill my empty arms.
Doors slam shut leaving echoes on a phone.
Goodbye... Were you trying to be kind?
You did your job well though,
No scar remains to flaw my useless breast,
Only a small death lies somewhere
Deep inside, beyond the surgeon's eye.

happiness

To come upon a sheltered cove tucked in the Devon coast
Surrounded by trees and softly rounded hills of
Rich green fields folding to the cliff's edge.
While on the shore, great rocks emerge with each outgoing

Tide, through which in swirling gullies seaweeds sway
In sensuous dance, while pools alive with darting life
Soon settle into darker mirrors of the flawless sky.
Waves with their old ebb and flow

Beat green and white upon indomitable stones,
Hypnotising with their splash and crawl.
Legs more used to city streets, suddenly
Clamber nimbly across small chasms

Finding footholds, reaching onwards
To new exciting peaks and then triumphant
You sit and watch the waters, as they
Curl around the sculptured island rock.

Far out the sea is shimmering silver in
The warm sun-salted air where curlews cry.
The nerve shattered world echoes out of reach
Just one harmonious thread of life is here,

Upon this magic time, everything complete.
Yet soon the winter storms must blast
This tranquil place, and you'll be far away.
No holding happiness of course, we know.
But hope is in the thought that such a thing exists
And may be found again one day, when we are ready.

a new puppy

She comes like a breeze
Into the sultry zones
Of exhaustion and worry,
Dispersing cobwebs of
Ritual and order.
Family trials of
Marital adjustment
Youthful self absorption
Geriatric demands
Get mitigated by
Her mindless beauty.
The old maternal whore
Rises from her grave afresh,
Enfolds her wagging,
Licking, frenzied bundle of affection
Appetite and fur,
Wantonly caught up again
In the new pulse of life.

richmond park

A place to go when marriages have broken
When London flats close in and
Children long to run and play;
To take new lovers in their open cars
Full of delight and young at heart;

A space to breath in when your world's askew
And you don't know where to turn or what to do;
For new babies in prams with doting parents,
School holidays.... interminably long.
Weekends when the stress of work

Has made your nerves like jumping frogs,
Heaven on earth for a multitude of dogs.
For walking gently when your young have gone;
And you can finally stop and stare.
After funerals or family rows,

When worries about those you love
Have made you mad, or sick or sad,
This place is always there.
Tall grasses shine with dew,
Narrow paths wind through soft

Unfurling brackens, while trees
Crisp salad greens in the clear
Spring light, stand in straggling woods
And copses, leading down to the lake's edge,
Where among the reeds wild birds dance and dive.

Then up across a gentle slope
Through wooded glade until you find a ridge
Where views go on and on to distant hills,
And people sit and rest on summer days
Feeling the cool breezes and sipping tea.

Hidden away a secret garden where
Azaleas, hydrangeas, begonias bloom
In thick profusion; streams speed their
Silken way through worlds of luxurious colours
Of flame red and mauve.

Small bridges span the chattering waters
To the wood's edge where ponds form
And black swan glide.
In dark circles of shade deer lie
Or skim leaping one after the other

Across the narrow roads.
Antlers emerge suddenly over the bracken tops,
And in the rutting season, fights
For who will rule the herd.
Like sabres their antlers crash and thrust

While ever gentle doe stands by,
Part of the wild and timeless scene.
When summer ends, leaves cover the space
In golden light and all are warm
Wood tones, a mellow russet canopy.

Squirrel chasing dogs, cantering horses,
Smoky air tinged with exciting feel of change.
When winter battens down at last
Dark skeletons remain and
Bitter winds rush over the causeway.

Ponds have waves of bobbing ducks,
And geese which muffled children feed from bags.
Until one day their eyes grow wide, as
Fairyland is there and all its
Glittery magic covers every leaf and tree.

life force

Windless marshes, broken bough among the reeds
You are there.
Bird fallen from sky onto sun baked shore
You are there.
Terrible rain swamping swollen banks
There you are.
Cries in the Cathedral, echoes on cold stone
There you are.
Swirl of the river at dusk, when fishes fly
There are you.
Reflections in the pool of the eye
There you are.
Struggling in the breathless blue moment of birth
There you are.
Consuming desire before the calm
You are there.
True as the kiss beyond love
There you are.
Timeless beyond the coil of senses
There are you...

the house

When the cat claw of despair runs deep
On a drizzle grey January day,
Swallowing me in it's bleak mid winter gloom,
I wrap my house around me like a cloak,
Drawing strength from it's protection.
Twenty years or more I've travelled on
Within it's solid frame,
Traumas and despair
As well as good times
Have been here.
As with a friend it offers hope,
Familiarity it's strongest suit.
Colours, patterns, light and shade
Whether by an open fire, mellowed by it's glow,
Or in the early hours while others sleep
I walk alone through empty rooms,
The unseen ghosts are friendly
Harmony prevails and I know
I am contained in a good place.

famine

My little brother cries
I cannot stop him.
He is stiff in my arms
Calling for his Mother.
But I have no breasts,
My body cannot give him
The thing he needs.
I want her too, but she sleeps
Such a deep sleep,
And does not answer
When I call her name.

She laid him on my lap,
Her eyes so strange and sad,
And now he shrieks and howls.
My Father sits as though
I was not there; perhaps
He cannot see me, or
Does not want to now.
He is so tired and thin
He only wants, it seems,
To sleep forever...

bangladesh
cyclone

A Young Boy.

Everywhere there is wetness.
No people are around.
Only the dogs circle
Round and round the
Bodies that are fallen
In the mud.

I am lifted suddenly,
Up into dry arms.
They say something
That sounds like
"My God he's lucky."
But I do not know
What they say,
Cannot understand
What they mean.

in memory of
an old dog

Shining prune eyes
Fixed upon my face
My ancient crusty cairn
Will sit for hours

When not oblivious
Underneath my desk
No frivolous dog is he
He favours only two or three

Gushing women he regards
with piteous scorn
His most exuberant display
Reserved for workmen

Strong on sweat
Especially if they wear a hat.
In far off days
He would out run

The swiftest child or beast
Make bids at chasing deer
Horses and police
He tipped a model

From her horse
Into a stagnant pond
While cameramen
Rushed to her aid,

He gobbled up
The ducks' stale bread,
Of which he is
Inordinately fond.

The days of daring deeds
Are now far gone,
And walks, though much enjoyed,
Can catch one out

On wind and limb.
Eyes and ears not
What they were,
One can get lost

If mistress strays too far.
Social life can be a strain
With aged dog around.
His loud and whistling snores

Make talking hard,
And dreadful pongs abound.
Other dogs are quite OK
Going at his pace

But puppies towering over him
Are kept well in their place.
Strangers at the door step back
At his ferocious bark.

But once inside
He licks their hands
Then bored,
Goes back to sleep.

This dignified and wise old dog,
Good, bad or muddy,
Has got me well and truly caught,
He is my greatest buddy.

the scream

Uncaring as winter, grey chill
Forms around your skull as you
Walk alone on hard earth,
Through empty woods, anger
Quickening your steps.
Deflating, weaving into
Aching despair. Where now,
Philosophy, quiet moments
Of enlightenment. Dead as
Trees up-ended in storm,
Roots naked to unpitying skies.
So must you scream, before you dance
Again, scream loud, before you can
Transmute the shuddering pain, into
Something with the shine of hope.

my young self

Falling in love
Was my thing.
The ambrosial fix,
A state of such
Mystical high
That anyone walking by,
So it seems to me now,
On a certain day
Could be embroiled
In my fantasy.

I had a talent for it.
The shaking legs
Thumping heart
Sleepless nights,
The unattainable
My speciality.
Happily married men
Gay boys, religious
Devoted to their mothers.

Wild winds of emotions
Swept my soul
At the slightest glance
Inflection of the voice.
Hope, they say
On swallow's wing
Makes lesser mortal king.
Me, I was a goddess.

the garden

Quietly resting now, the garden
Having seen more hectic days,
Football on a battered lawn
Sandpit, slides, bonfire night
Children running up and down

A space to show exuberance.
Now things have settled down,
Have come of age,
A haven full of gentleness.
Clematis and honeysuckle

Spill around its edges,
Butterflies, bees, buddleia
In purple profusion mingle
With japonica, geranium, lavender,
An oasis of colour

And gently scented air.
An ancient dog, stiff-legged
Finds comfort on the grass
Beneath magnolia trees,
While ferns, nasturtiums, lobelia

Tumble across the paths
Making nests in which an even
Older cat may snooze sun-baked.
Birds make brave bids for their bath
Splashing roses in the hustle,

Stealthily nibbling grapes from off the vine.
laburnum, philadelphus give shade
In the hot afternoon.
Concorde's blast now and again
Brings the world with all its thrill

Like a high wind through a glade.
But soon the sound of birds
And buzzing bee predominates.
The garden reigns once more
In all it's tranquil loveliness.

understanding

In deep night you came alone
Soft your tread on rocky shore.
Here, I cried, I'm here.
But clouded moon obscured.
Urgent calling, then belated
Fearing that you would not hear.
The waves laughed at my naked child
Back to your cradle...cradle.
Let the rocking make you sleep.
And I wept in the night's core
While fishes played.
Time, then dawn on the bare sands,
The ebb of tide, little pools alive.
I found so close entwined we lay
Your heart on mine
The sun came over the dark earth
And it was day.

love

Beyond the deepest well my knowing of you goes
As waves know when to break or
Birds to change their course,
As ferns uncurl and new born babies cry,
Dissolving crystals on a mountain peak
Or clouds to flee the sky,
As honey from the bee or falling rain to cease,
I find my home in you and peace.
Knowing you so deeply, I know you not at all
In ways that many lovers know,
Or even that you care to know I live.
So I must leave it there,
Knowing only that you are,
And lost in you all things
Come right in the end.

the day
you leave
hospital

The day you leave the hospital
With its lines of tidy beds,
Brave smiles, disinfectant smells,
The swish of nurses as they go about
Their tasks, footsteps echoing along corridors
Small intimacies with strangers
Sudden drama round a bed.
Thoughtful eyes as doctors stare
A little longer than is comfortable.
Cheerful noisy cleaners from sunnier climes,
Early morning brightness and the clink of spoons
At dawn, or so it seems.
The fear and the relief on other patients' faces
Which you know must show as blatantly upon your own,
You walk a little faster to your own front door,
The day you leave the hospital.

The day you leave the hospital
The air is sweet with honeysuckle and roses
In the late summer day.
The sky was never quite so huge
Or a boiled egg taste so good.

Your house is a like a castle of
Luxury and taste and like a mistress
Bathed, scented, waiting her lover's call,
You glide about touching things in sensuous delight
And all the mundane chores, routines
Take on a different hue,
While free as light and wide awake
You'll really live, appreciate
The people in your life every single day
From now on you say, on
The day you leave the hospital

depression

A leaden sea
blocking air
crushing
forcing you under
its mountainous grey mass
enveloping
pervading
tunnelling
into your belly
behind your eyes
seeping dark sludge through the brain
extinguishing

light

cards
in the afternoon

There they sit in their fours, sensibly
Around the green baize table.
Winter, Summer, Autumn, Spring.
Neat, tidy grey hair tastefully tinted.

Not too much make up or overmuch
Style, middle class modulated voices
Creaming off the day's news, spectacles
At the ready, awaiting their turn

For the day's play. "One heart
Two diamonds, three clubs" they say,
"Three no trumps" and they're away.
Widows forget they must go home

Alone to empty flats and locking up.
Palpitations in the night, acid taste
Of loneliness at dawn. Wives let go a
Partner's unreasonable demands,

Selfish bullying. A grandchild's
Cot death. A daughter's sad face.
Pains in their heads, in their arms
And their legs. The biopsy next week

That might be fatal, the dearly
Loved husband who is slowly dying.
The selfish in-law, who is endlessly
Trying. Into the pool of oblivion they go.

Bidding grand slams, then going down
They straighten their backs and deal
Again. "Sorry partner, It couldn't be made.
"If you'd led a diamond".

"But I wanted a spade." Then respite as
they stop for tea, sandwiches with every
Filling. Cakes from M&S and biscuits,
For those abandoning all hope

Of slimming. There they sit in
Their fours sensibly, around the green
Baize table. Winter, Summer, Autumn, Spring.
True refuge, comfort there to be found.

Grateful that what ever else
May lie ahead, they can still come
And play, find hope every day,
With cards in the afternoon.

thoughts about death

Reincarnation, oblivion,
Eternal spirit mingle.

Strange bed fellows,
Mystic, scientist

Battle out their themes.
Disease, disintegration

Of our mortal selves -
The dreaded loss.

If, or where
The spirit soars,

The question rises
Into space unanswered.

Only when beauty smudges
From eyes, hair, limbs,

Hills become mountains
Friends become senile,

Our gut reaction catches up
Unmasked fear is there.

Those few you love
And leave behind,

Will find that anything
That is real, true in you

Will still be theirs.
Any gift unhampered

By your absence.
Heaven, at least in part

Must surely be
A quiet mind, at

Infinite peace with itself.
So, when the time comes

Death, extinguish the shadows
Of a life punch drunk

With care; let me fall
Into your embrace unafraid.

breakdown

We cannot bear another's suffering,
Lift it like a camel over the parched
Tracks of their experience.
Only they can choose the course to
Whatever rich reward or desolation
May engulf the human heart and mind.
Yet like some signpost on the way
We simply can be there,
Loving and unwavering, so through
The confusion of their minds' despair
They see us wait. They must
Negotiate the barren way alone.
We must not stumble after them
And too get lost.

swan
in winter

In the faded sun, a winter white swan
Finds haven from the wild Icelandic shore,
Driven on her beating wings she came
Across the ocean's roar to this clear spot.
Fighting wind and mist
Spurred by her quest for continuity
A peaceful lake where she can glide among the reeds
At home, safe with her own kind.
Lovely bird, how calm you seem.
No two edged imagination blights your days,
Not for you those trigger words to hell,
They do not stop you sleeping

Your elegant neck outcraned
into your warm and feathered body.
Words cannot destroy, make you cry.
Famine, Aids, Nuclear war.
No horrendous scream within is triggered
By their shattering implications.
You cannot see, strange bird,
That humans skid into the path
Of their own destruction.
Winter white swan in the faded sun
Serenely graceful on the lake.

my father

Out of the misty melancholy bogs
His gentle humour sprang.
Poet, soldier, man of law
Softly telling tales of witches.
From the child's view
Hairs inside his nose,
Knees, bony, uncuddlesome.
Serious in play, you rose
To his approval, no down
On all fours Dad was he.
Yet, he it was who saw
The night was not too dark
For your young heart to bear.
Scary wind or rattling door
All explained away.
Perhaps he hugged me once,
I cannot now recall, only
The hue of his eyes as
Deep and mournful
As an Irish lake, remains.

mourning the loss of christian faith

In your absence, the soul blanched
Colourless as on the morning of birth,
Cord broken, bruised, bare, expelled
From the womb craving sustenance
In order to make plausible our
Shambling blink of time.
Yet it must be if you are gone
So too is part of me, for you
Were woven into my being from the start.
Your ghost will follow to the grave
Lighting a path we cannot all negotiate.
Hope is what you offered.
Yours are the arms holding drunken tramps,
Healing the smelling sores of Calcutta.
Keeping families united,
Caring for the unborn child,
Protecting redundant old bodies.
You cry forgiveness for failure
For falling like a leper by the way.
Yours the incense, the genuflexion,
Papal pomp, lighted candle in a country church.
In you is certainty, your standards unchanging,
Good and evil not things to argue about.
Inspiration for man's highest achievements
Spawned by your existence,
As well as agonies of guilt.
Oh, good wise Godly man,
If we cannot now follow your every word,
Let us not close irrevocably, doors
That open on to higher selves,
Touching basic simple truths so magically.

the fool's hour

In the fool's hour
Passion is flown
No cosmic charge or
flagrant burn-out left
Body's pawn, no longer.
Free now for a wealth
Of cerebral delights.
Books, music,
Philosophic heights.

Along the sea's edge
Into the summer night
Free as the waves that
Lilt against the shore.
Over and gone
Finished forever
Those lusty couplings,
Yearning affairs,
No more, no more.
Growing old will be peaceful.

In the fool's hour
A small flamenco
Starts inside your heart,
As the young man smiles
Searching in your eyes
For things he has not yet
Had time to find.
And in the fool's hour
You are young again.